Copyrighted Material

No part of this publication may be reproduced in whole or in part, or stored in a retrieval system, or transmitted in any form or by any means, electronic, mechanical, photography, recording, or otherwise, without written permission of the publisher. For information regarding permission, please email Jessica Watson at fourplusanangel@gmail.com.

©2016 by Jessica Watson, Author
©2016 by Johi Kokjohn-Wagner, Illustrator
Layout/Design by Marsha Hobert

ISBN-13: 978-0990982500
ISBN-10: 0990982505
BISAC: Juvenile Fiction / Family / New Baby

Published in the U.S.A.

All rights reserved.

This book belongs to:

_____

Due Date: _____
Birth Date: _____

Dedicated to Hadley Jane

Written by Jessica Watson
Illustrated by Johi Kokjohn-Wagner

We wondered what you would look like,

a smile like Mommy

or eyes like Daddy?

You would be here someday soon.

as we whispered to you.

You decided to come so very soon.

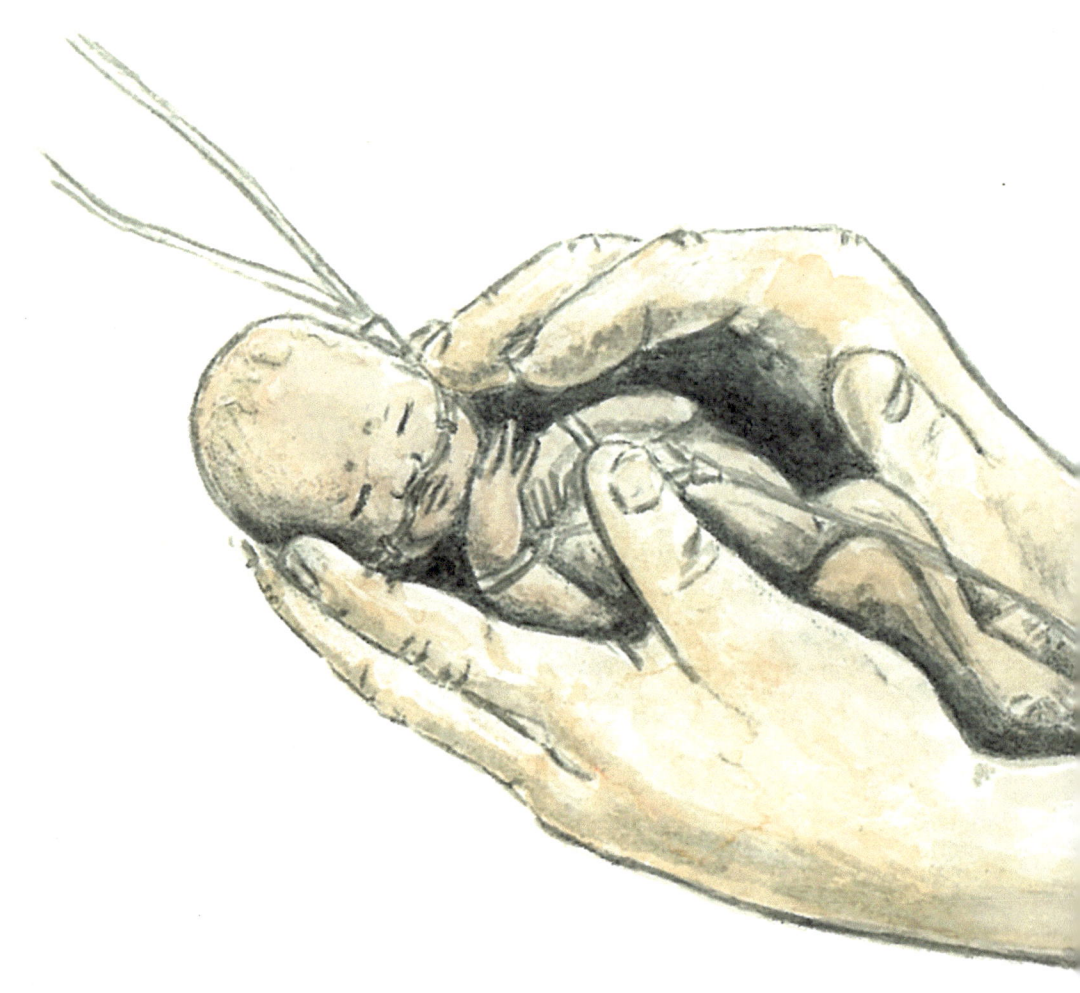

You fit right
into your daddy's hand
so you stayed at the hospital to grow,
but you would be bigger soon.

and we watched and we waited.

You would be growing soon.

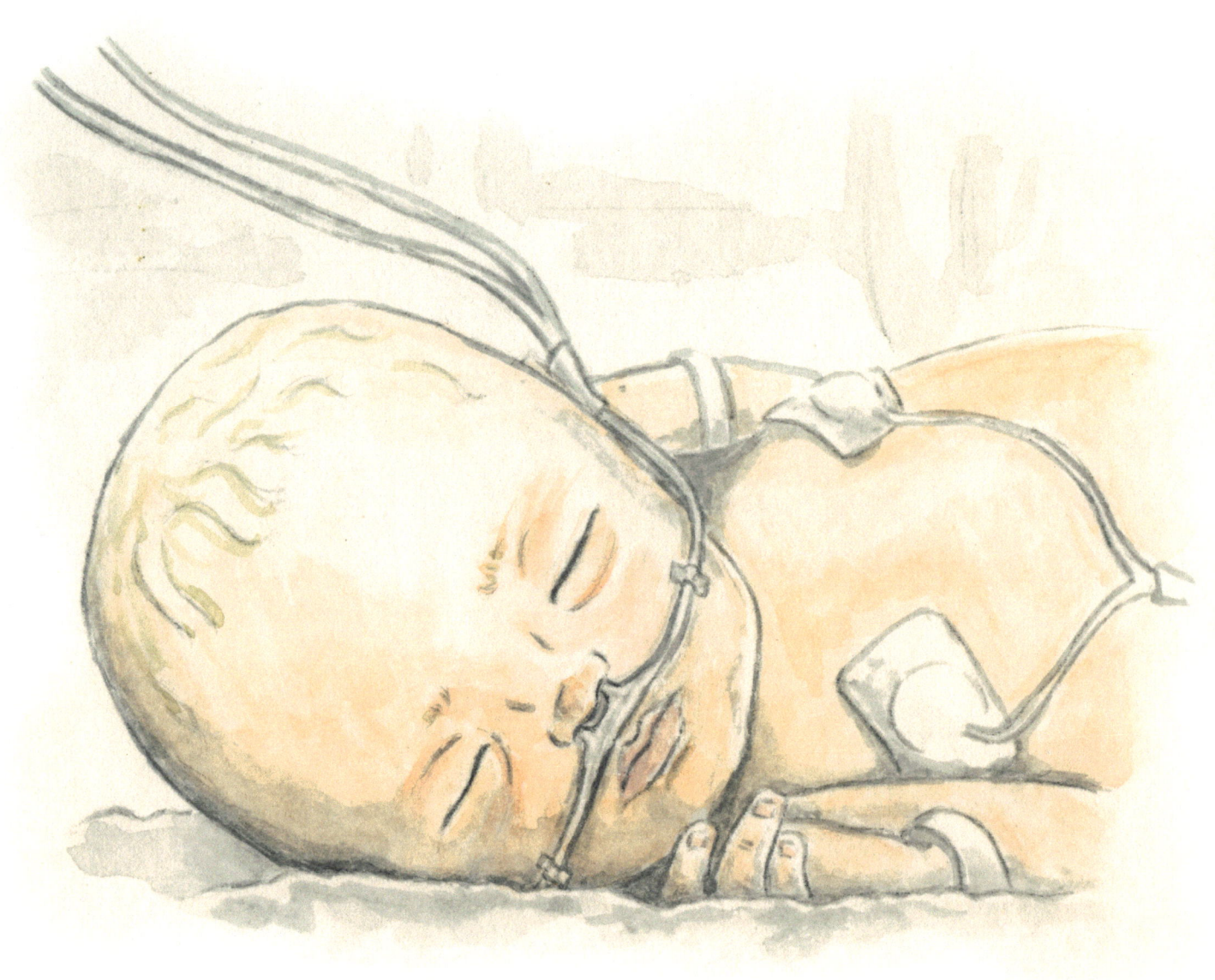

You learned important baby things ...

how to stay warm and how to breathe by yourself.

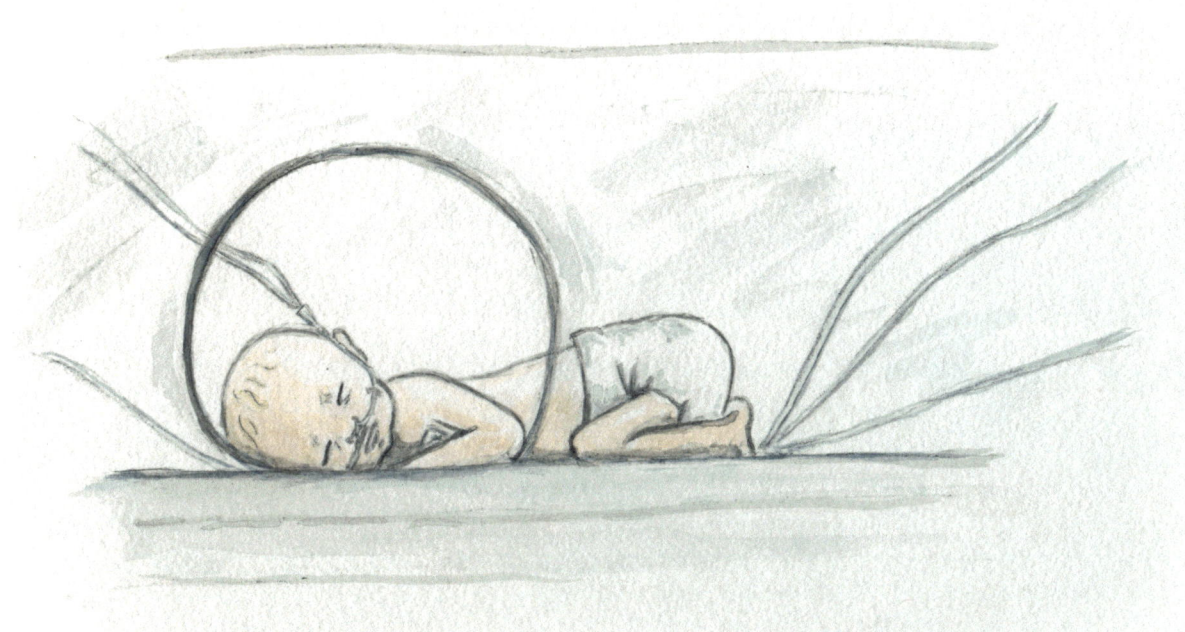

You would be stronger soon.

We reached our hands
into your little space

and held your fingers or
touched your toes.

We would hold you to
our hearts soon.

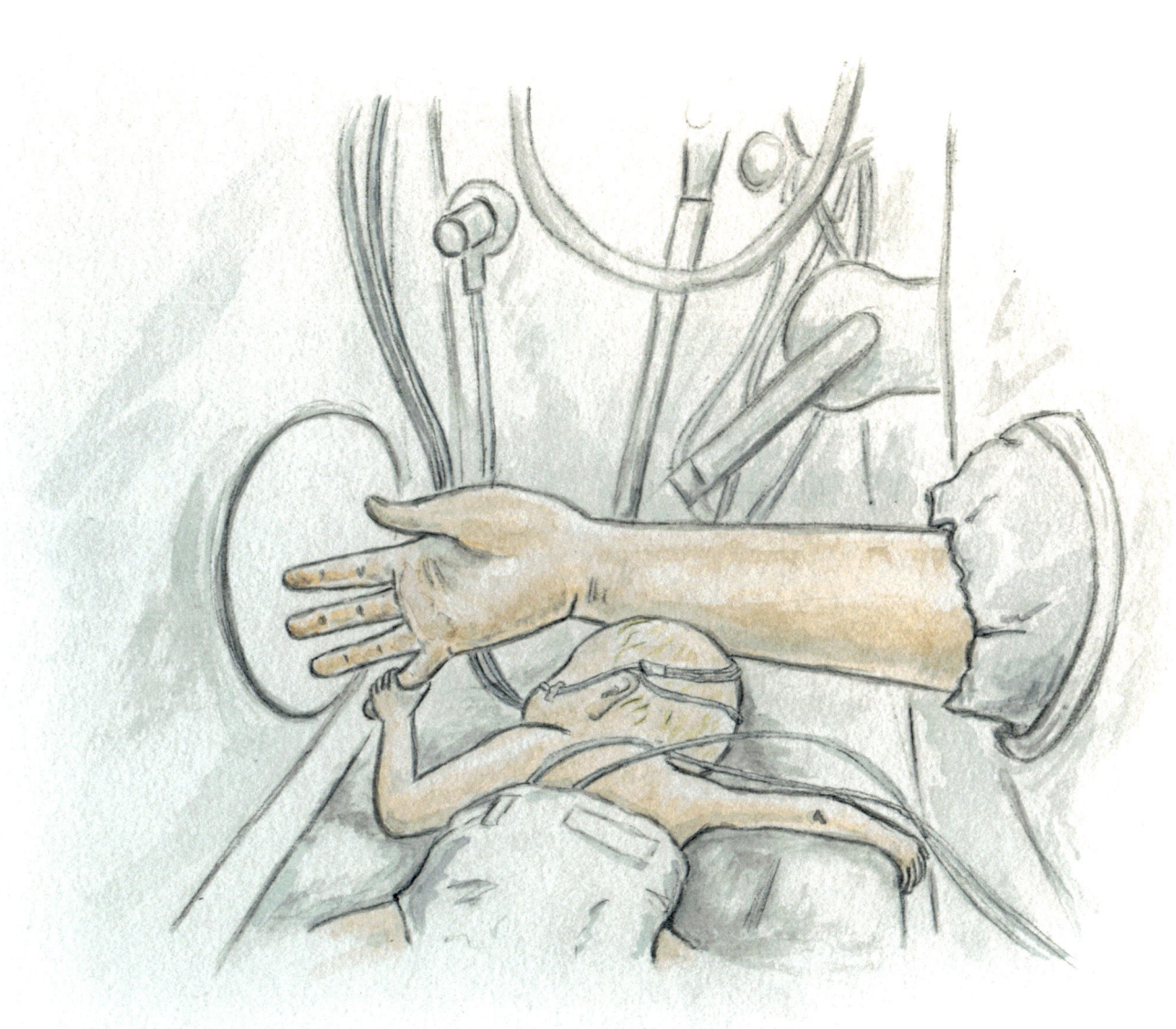

The doctors said you would be ready soon.

We lifted you from your hospital bed one last time

and held up the tiniest of clothes.

You would be wearing them soon.

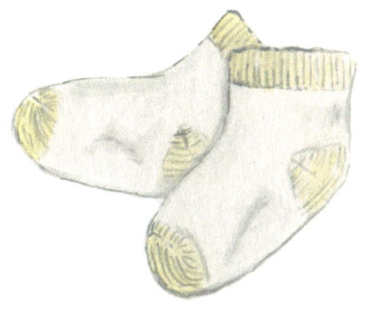

We brought you home,
right where you belong.

Where we watch
you grow from very
small to very tall,

and remember the day
 you came a little bit too soon.

Made in the USA
Columbia, SC
05 May 2025